GW00363193

UK price
£6.95

THE CREATIVE BOOK OF

Party Decorations

THE CREATIVE BOOK OF

Party Decorations

Suzie Major

Published by Salamander Books Limited
LONDON ● NEW YORK

Published by Salamander Books Ltd.,
52 Bedford Row,
London WC1R 4LR,
England.

©Salamander Books Ltd. 1987
ISBN 0 86101 329 8

Distributed by Hodder and Stoughton Services,
PO Box 6, Mill Road, Dunton Green,
Sevenoaks, Kent TN13 2XX.

CREDITS

Editor-in-chief: Jilly Glassborow

Editor: Eleanor Van Zandt

Designer: Kathy Gummer

Photographer: Terry Dilliway

Line artwork: New Leaf Designs

Typeset by: The Old Mill, London

Colour separation by: Fotographics Ltd, London – Hong Kong

Printed in Italy

CONTENTS

─── *INTRODUCTION* ───

There's always an excuse for a party, whether it is a birthday, an anniversary, Christmas, or Halloween, or the celebration of something extra special such as the birth of a new baby, a graduation or a wedding. What better way to make the occasion go with a swing than to make your own festive decorations!

You can produce stunning effects at a low cost, and in the colours and styles to suit your décor. This book shows you how, from the very simplest paper chains and masks for children to make, up to more complicated cut-outs, stylish party hats and fake trees. Each item is accompanied by colourful step-by-step photographs and detailed but easy-to-follow instructions, showing you how to put the finished article together from basic materials. Where possible, we have included templates for shapes that are difficult to draw freehand. These can be found at the back of the book.

There is something here for every occasion, and many of the decorations can be adapted to suit a different theme, with the use of a different colour or material. Experiment a little with them ... and have a wonderful party!

GARLANDS

Garlands take many forms, and although the name may suggest greenery or flowers, they are basically anything that can be strung from one place to another, on walls or ceilings or across the furniture. This includes paper chains, cut-outs in all shapes, fresh foliage and flowers, and garlands made from tinsel and foil, or even from fabrics.

You can take any of these and adapt them to your chosen party theme: eggs and chicks for Easter, witches for Halloween, hearts for Valentine's Day, trees and stars for Christmas. Many are simple enough for children to make themselves for their own parties.

This beautiful garland can be made any time of the year; just use whatever foliage is in season and either real or silk flowers. Take three lengths of string and knot them together at regular intervals of about 20-25cm (8-10in). Using contrasting thread or paper clips, mark the points from which the garland will be hung and to which ribbon will be attached.

Tie short lengths of florist's wire to small bunches of foliage. Then start twisting the foliage onto the string, working from both ends so that the garland looks symmetrical. Intersperse the foliage with wired bunches of flowers.

Wire on lengths of wide satin or gift wrap ribbon as you come to the marked points. Keep on adding small wired bunches of fresh foliage, silk flowers and ribbon from both ends, until they meet in the middle.

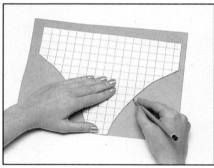

A frisky line of red and black undies, decorated with tinsel, lace, glitter, zips, even pom-poms ... great fun for a stag party! Substitute wicked jockey shorts for a girls-only night. Make a pattern from graph paper, and mark out the knicker shapes on cartridge (heavy drawing) paper or coloured cardboard — as many as you like.

Cut out the shapes and decorate them with your chosen materials: sticky-backed plastic, felt, foil, satin, etc. Then add the finishing touches with oddments of lace, ribbon, and, for an extra bit of glamour, tinsel and glitter.

Use a long piece of lace or ribbon to string the knickers together, sticking it to the back of each cut-out with glue or double-sided tape.

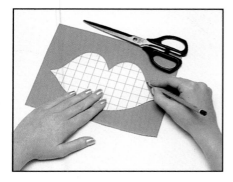

L uscious lips to show your sweetheart how much you love him on Valentine's Day or your anniversary. You will need a piece of fluorescent pink craft paper 76 by 12.5cm (30 by 5in). You should be able to get four strips this size out of a standard sheet of craft paper. Draw a lips shape (using folded paper will ensure symmetry) and cut it out in cardboard.

Fold the paper in half from right to left, and then from right to left again. This will give you four sets of lips. Place the pattern on top and draw round it, making sure that the pattern meets each side; otherwise the lips won't hold together.

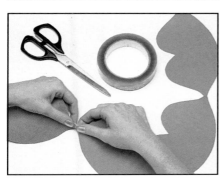

Cut out the shape using sharp scissors. Join each set of lips together at the ends to make one long garland.

For each heart cut out two shapes in scarlet satin, using the template on page 118. Placing right sides together, sew around the edges, taking only a very small seam allowance and leaving a small gap at the top for turning it right side out.

Turn the heart right side out and stuff it carefully with polyester filling. Then neatly sew up the gap. Trim each heart with a strip of silver ribbon down the middle and a silver bow on the top. Attach the hearts to a strip of wide red satin ribbon.

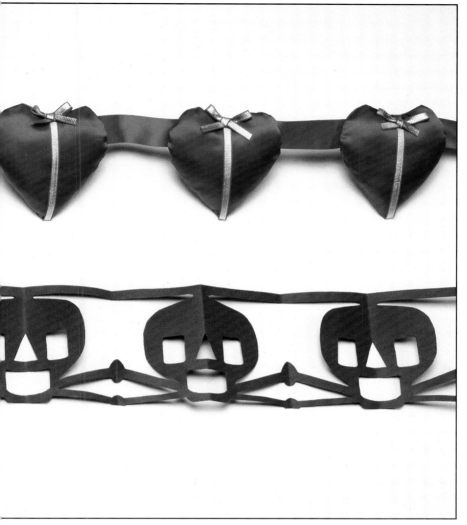

This garland is easy to make for a Halloween or fancy dress party. First take long strips of black paper, measuring 105 by 75cm (40 by 30in) each. You may need to buy a roll of paper to get the length you require. Fold each strip in half from right to left, three times.

Trace and cut out the template given on page 118 and use it to trace the shape onto the folded strip. Cut out the shape carefully with sharp scissors. Open out the strip, and join each strip to the next with a little sticky tape at the edges.

This is a lovely decoration for a wedding table and makes the most of a crisp white tablecloth. Begin by taking some large white wooden rings — the kind used on curtain poles — and winding ribbon around them as shown.

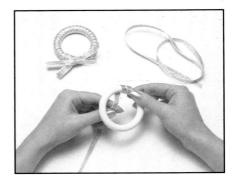

Tie a bow at the top to hide the little metal ring, then pin each one to the front overhang of the tablecloth, spacing them evenly. Thread through a length of net, bunching it between the rings to make a good swag.

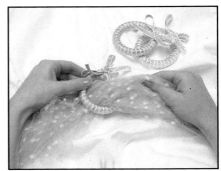

When the net is evenly arranged, attach strips of curling gift wrap ribbon to the lower edge of each ring as a finishing touch. Curl the ribbon by running the blunt edge of a pair of scissors along it.

The paper used for these crackers is similar in texture to curling gift wrap ribbon and has a lovely shiny satin finish. Cover empty toilet paper rolls or cardboard tubes with white sticky-backed plastic, which prevents the colour from showing through. Now cut pieces of shiny paper, twice as long as the tubes, and wide enough to go easily around them.

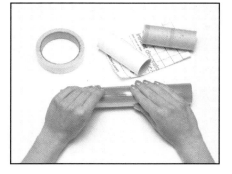

Wrap the tube in the paper and fix in place with double-sided tape. Don't twist the ends; scrunch them in with elastic (rubber) bands, which you can then cover with strips of curling ribbon. Decorate the crackers with boiled sweets (hard candies), stuck on with double-sided tape. Staple the crackers onto a strip of tinsel and trim the garland with sweets and baubles.

This is a fun and simple way to hang up your Christmas cards. Simply take three long pieces of gift wrap or woven ribbon in red, green and gold, and plait them tightly together. Knot them at each end to hold them in place.

Now take some clothes pegs, lay them on several sheets of newspaper and spray them with gold paint. Turn them until all the sides have been covered and leave them to dry.

Fasten the ribbon to the wall at each end, and use the gold pegs to attach your Christmas cards to it. (If you prefer, and if you have some to spare, you could use tinsel instead of ribbon.)

Here is a lovely sparkly garland to hang at Christmastime. If you want to make it for a birthday party instead, substitute little boxed gifts and bottles for the bells, and make trees in pastel colours. Cut the chosen shapes from foil-covered cardboard, marking them out on the wrong side. Be careful when cutting as foil cardboard tends to crinkle at the edges.

Make a tiny hole in the top of each, using a hole punch, or the tip of a skewer. Using red twine, tie each shape to a long strand of tinsel, leaving even spaces between them. At the top of each bell, fix a bow of gold-covered wire; on the trees, a little star.

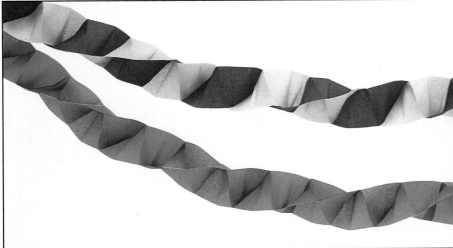

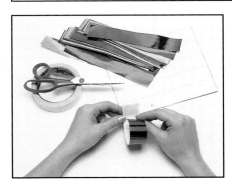

Bright-coloured foil paper makes a festive version of the simple link chain. Begin by cutting lots of strips about 18 by 3cm (7 by 1¼in). Stick the ends of the first strip together with double-sided tape (neater and quicker than glue) to make a link.

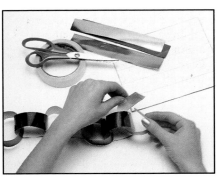

Now simply thread the next strip through and stick the ends together. Continue in this way, alternating the colours, until the chain is as long as you want it.

This simple paper chain takes only a few minutes to make. All you need are two different-coloured crepe papers and a touch of glue. Cut 7.5cm (3in) off the end of each crepe paper roll. Place the strips at right angles to each other, and glue one end over the other as shown.

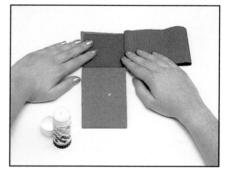

Bring the lower strip up and fold it over the other, then fold the right-hand strip over to the left as shown.

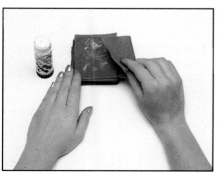

That's all there is to it; just keep folding the strips over each other alternately until you reach the end. Glue them together at the ends and trim off any extra bits.

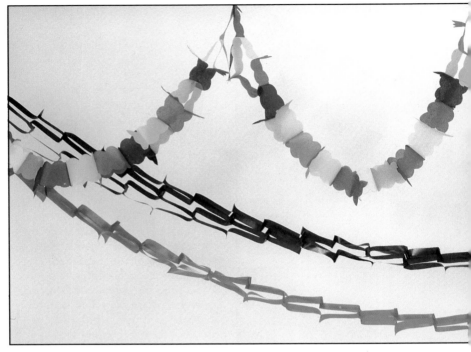

This variation on the standard pull-out chain is rectangular and has scalloped edges. It is very simple to make, though. Using the template on page 118, cut out lots of tissue shapes in different colours and mix them up for a random, multicoloured effect.

All you need to do now is glue them together. Take the first two and stick them centre to centre.

Now take another piece and glue it to one of the first pieces at each end. Continue gluing, alternately centre-to-centre and end-to-end, until the chain is the required length.

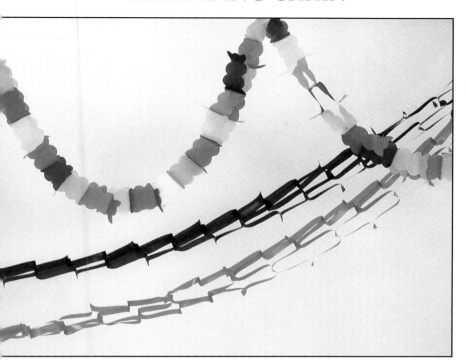

This traditional Christmas paper chain is easy to make and is shown cut from a waxed paper, which is stronger than ordinary tissue. First take a sheet of paper measuring about 50 by 35cm (20 by 14in) and fold it into four lengthwise.

Now make evenly spaced cuts all along one edge, stopping about 1.5cm (½in) from the other side. Turn the paper around and make additional cuts between the first set, again stopping short of the edge.

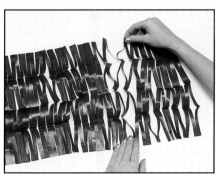

Open the chain out carefully. If you wish, you can glue the ends of two chains together to make a longer one. If your chain sags too much, string some thread through the top links to hold it together.

This graceful paper chain is made from circular pieces of tissue paper. First cut two circles of cardboard and lots of circles of tissue paper, all 10cm (4in) in diameter. Take about ten tissue paper circles and fold them together in four. If you use more than about ten layers, the folds won't be as good.

Now make two curved cuts as shown, from the single-folded edge almost to the double folds. Open out the circles. Glue the centre of the first circle to the middle of one cardboard circle.

Next, take the second tissue circle and glue it to the first at the top and bottom. Glue the third circle to the centre of the second circle. Continue in this way, remembering to glue alternate circles in the same place at the top and bottom. If you alter the positioning you will spoil the effect. Finally glue the other cardboard circle to the last tissue circle to complete the garland.

A nother simple garland made from tissue paper. Cut out a cardboard pattern from the template on page 118. Now cut out lots of flower shapes from tissue paper, using several different colours.

To start the garland, dab a little glue (one that won't soak through the thin paper) onto alternate petals of the first flower. Place the second flower on top and press them together.

Now on the second flower dab glue on the petals lying between those glued on the first flower. Take the third flower and press it firmly on top. Continue in this way, gluing petals in alternate positions, until the garland is long enough. Cut two extra cardboard shapes from the pattern and glue them to either end. Onto these tape a little loop of cord for hanging the garland.

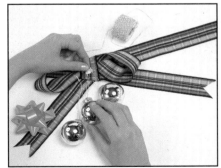

For those with a sugary tooth, here is a garland covered in brightly wrapped sweets — to be enjoyed long after the party is over. Cut a length of ribbon about 135cm (54in) long and mark the centre. Next cut three 112cm (45in) lengths of ribbon and make them up into three bows, stapling the loops into an open position as shown and trimming the ends into points.

Tape the bows onto each end and onto the centre of the main ribbon length. Then use silver thread to hang clusters of baubles from the centre of the bows. (Hang the baubles at varying lengths for the best effect.) Glue the threads to the centre of the bows and cover them up with an adhesive ribbon rosette.

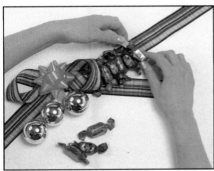

Decorate some sweets with silver stars and staple them along the top edge of the ribbon between the bows. Use double-sided tape to attach the underside of the sweets to the ribbon. Finally, sew curtain rings onto the back of the ribbon for hanging the garland.

For the rosettes, cut a circle of silver cardboard, 10cm (4in) across. Take a piece of ribbon 80cm (32in) long, fold it in half and staple it to the centre of the circle. Trim the ribbon ends into points. Staple the sweets in a circle around the cardboard as shown, then stick a ribbon star in the centre. Using sticky tape, attach a curtain ring to the back of the circle for hanging up the rosette.

If a young member of the family has just graduated from college or university, throw a party for him or her, and hang a graduation garland of mortarboards on the wall. First cut out 20cm (8in) squares from foil cardboard or ordinary cardboard covered in foil paper. Stick shiny tape around the edges of each square.

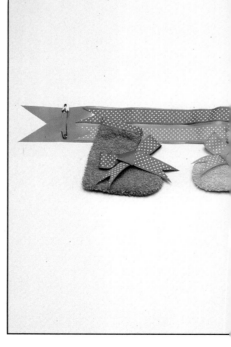

Next turn each square over and mark two diagonal pencil lines across it as shown. Where they meet in the centre, pierce a small hole. Push a tassel (see page 126 for instructions) through the front, and tape it in place. Now make a hole in one corner and attach each mortarboard to a length of tinsel, tying it with a small piece of gold-covered wire.

BOOTEE GARLAND

Pin this clever garland to the front of the table at a christening party. First cut bootee shapes from pink and blue towelling fabric (terrycloth) — two for each bootee. Next, cut strips of pink and blue spotted ribbon to fit the top edge of each bootee shape. Press them in half and then pin and tack (baste) them to the tops of the bootees. Stitch them in place.

Now sew the front and back of each bootee together, around the edge, with right sides facing. Trim the seam and turn the bootee right side out. Attach a bow in matching ribbon.

Cut a length of wide ribbon and trim it with pink and blue spotted ribbon using double-sided tape. Pin the bootees to the ribbon as shown. To hang the garland, fix a large safety pin at each end, so that you can pin or hook it in place.

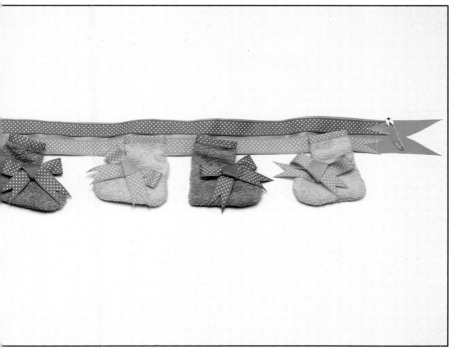

— HANGING DECORATIONS —

Whatever the occasion, some attractive decorations hanging on the walls or from the ceiling will add sparkle to a party. This section covers all kinds, from wreaths to mobiles.

Wreaths can be hung from doors, walls or the mantelpiece and can be made from ribbons and fabrics as well as from fresh or dried foliage. Other attractive hanging decorations include such things as kites and balloons for children's parties, fans and bows for grown-up affairs, such as weddings and anniversaries, and tinsel shapes for Christmas. Mobiles are simple to make and can be adapted for every occasion.

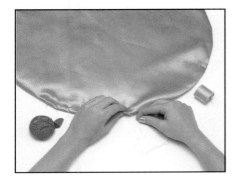

T his jolly wall hanging can be folded up in a drawer and brought out every Halloween. Cut out two satin shapes, using the template on page 119. Place right sides together, and sew around the edge, leaving the flat part at the bottom open. Turn the shape right side out, slip in a piece of medium-weight wadding (batting), and slipstich the gap together.

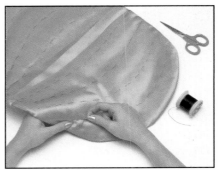

Mark the quilting lines with tacking (basting) stitches using dark thread. Now machine quilt, using a small zigzag stich and orange thread. If you haven't got a machine, a small backstitch will be fine. Remove the tacking when you have finished.

Cut out the eyes, mouth and stem in black and green felt, using the templates on page 119. The loop is another piece of felt, about 13cm (5in) long, which you sew under the edge of the stem. All the felt pieces are sewn on with a machined satin stitch using orange thread.

This Christmas wreath is based on a child's plastic hoop, and makes a delightful decoration for the wall or mantelpiece. First of all you need a plastic hoop; any size will do. Cut long strips of wadding (batting) and wind them around the hoop, holding the edges in place with sticky tape. We gave it two layers of medium-weight wadding.

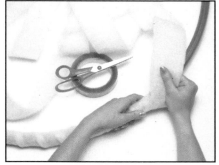

Next take some 8cm- (3in)-wide ribbon and wind it firmly around the hoop, in the opposite direction to the wadding. Make sure the wadding is entirely covered. Take a contrasting ribbon, about 6cm (2in) wide, and wrap it over the first ribbon, leaving equal spaces between the loops. Repeat with a third ribbon, 4cm (1½in) wide.

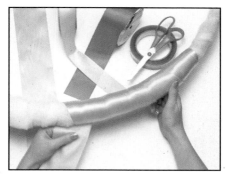

Make sure each ribbon starts and finishes in the same place so that all the joins are together. This will be the top of the hoop. Wind tinsel around the hoop, over the ribbons. Pin or staple a wide piece of ribbon over all the joins at the top. Tape a cluster of ribbon, tinsel, baubles and bells at the top and add a large bow to finish off.

Hang this traditional wreath on the front door to give a warm welcome to Christmastime callers. To begin, take a wire coathanger and pull it into a circle. Bend the hook down to form a loop.

Now wire together small bunches of holly, spruce and other foliage. Then attach each bunch to the circle. Be careful when handling the holly; you can get a bit scratched, and some people can come out in a rash from it. Keep going in one direction until the whole circle is covered.

On top of this add some wired pine cones and, for extra colour, some curly red ribbon. (Use curling gift wrap ribbon for this, running the blunt edge of a pair of scissors along it to make it curl.) Red holly berries look great if you can get hold of them, but they tend to drop very quickly, so they would need replacing often. Finish off with a big red satin bow.

Dried flowers and foliage make a lovely wreath that will last for ages. It is possible to make your own base for the wreath, but a florist should be able to provide you with a sturdy woven cane base, such as this one, for a small cost.

Wire up plenty of colourful flowers, either singly or in bunches, depending on their size. Allow plenty of wire for attaching them securely to the base. The flowers used here include strawflowers (or everlasting), yarrow and sea lavender.

Pine cones can easily be wired around the base. Choose small closed ones for the best effect. If it is the wrong time of year to collect the cones, your florist or a shop selling dried flowers will probably have some, and they should cost very little.

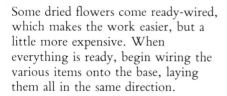

Some dried flowers come ready-wired, which makes the work easier, but a little more expensive. When everything is ready, begin wiring the various items onto the base, laying them all in the same direction.

Some flower heads will be very delicate and break off. If so, simply dab a little glue on the back and stick them on. If you start to run out of dried flowers, or you want to save some money, heather from the garden can be included; it will dry naturally once it is in place.

A large foil star to hang in the centre of the ceiling or over the fireplace. Try it out on a piece of ordinary paper first, as it is a little fiddly. Cut a piece of foil paper about 45cm (18in) square. Fold it in half from corner to corner, then in half twice again, making a small triangle.

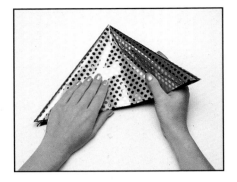

Bend the single-fold edge over to the edge with three folds. Open it out, and rule two lines from the corners at the base of the triangle to the centre crease. Cut along these two lines.

Refold the crease and rule two more lines, forming a small triangle as seen here. Cut this out. Now snip the point off and open the star out. Glue it to another piece of thicker foil paper for backing and cut the star out carefully when the glue has dried. Finish it off with a ribbon rosette in the centre.

This simple star can be hung on the wall or from the ceiling. First make the pattern for the star. Using a ruler and protractor, draw an equilateral triangle (each angle is 60°). Cut out the triangle and use it as a pattern to make another one. Then glue one triangle over the other to form the star. Use this pattern to cut a star from foil paper.

Fold the star in half three times between opposite points. Next fold it in half three times between opposite angles as shown. Every angle and point should now have a fold in it.

The star will now easily bend into its sculptured shape. Make a small hole in its top point with a hole punch or a skewer, then put some thread through the hole to hang it up.

This is a very effective fabric wreath, which can be brought out for Christmas year after year. All you need are three strips of fabric, in red, green and white, about 150cm (60in) long and 18cm (7in) wide. Sew them into tubes, right side facing, leaving one end open.

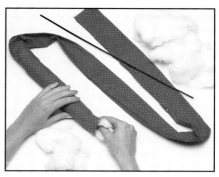

Turn each tube right side out and stuff it with polyester filling, polystyrene beads or old tights (pantyhose) cut into strips. Have a stick handy to help push the stuffing down the tube. Turn in the raw edges and sew them together.

Wind narrow red ribbon around the green tube, sewing it in place at each end to secure. When you have made all three tubes, plait them together loosely and join the ends together. Cover the point where they join with a large bow made from net, and add three small net bows around the ring.

Thread tinsel through the wreath, and decorate with golden baubles, tied on with thread at the back. To finish, add some curly strands of gold gift wrap ribbon. Curl the ribbon by running the blunt edge of a pair of scissors along it.

This decoration can be made with tissue paper, coloured aluminium foil, thin cardboard or construction paper. Cut between six and twelve bell shapes (depending on the thickness of the paper you use). Fold each shape in half and then open it out again.

Lay the cut-outs carefully on top of each other with all the creases in the centre. Now take a needle and thread, and starting at the top, make three long stitches down the middle. Bring the needle up and over the bottom to secure the shapes in place. Next make a small stitch between each long stitch. At the top, knot the two ends together.

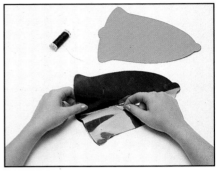

Ease the bell open, piece by piece, until it forms a rounded shape. You could easily do exactly the same thing with other shapes such as a heart, ball or tree.

FANCY FOIL

Make these shiny decorations from foil wrapping paper. Cut out eight circles in each of the following diameters: 9cm (3½in), 7.5cm (3in) and 6cm (2¼in). Then from cardboard cut out four circles 2cm (¾in) in diameter and two of 1.5cm (½in) for the centres. Fold the largest foil circles into quarters and staple four of them onto a large cardboard circle.

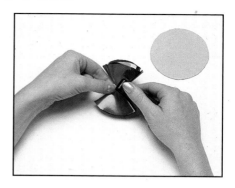

In the same way, staple the other four foil circles to another cardboard circle. Glue the two cardboard circles together with a string between them. Leave a long piece hanging below for the other two balls. Fluff out the edges of foil to make a good shape.

Now make the other two balls in the same way, using the smaller cardboard circles for the tiniest. Fix the balls to the string as you go.

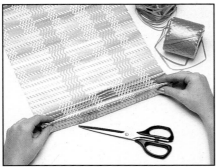

W hat could be simpler than these crisply-pleated paper fans, trimmed with curling ribbons? To begin, take a strip of printed wrapping paper and pleat it crosswise as shown.

When you have finished the folding, hold the fan together by stapling it at one end. Cut some strips of gift wrap ribbon and run them along the edge of a ruler, or over a scissors blade, so that they curl.

Slip the ends of the ribbons between the folds of the fan and staple them in place. Finish by fixing a ribbon rosette over the stapled end.

Hang these pretty net fans on the wall or on the corner of a mirror, or use them to decorate a tablecloth. They are made from strips of net about 30cm (12in) wide and 1 metre (40in) long. Cut two strips of each colour and concertina-fold them crosswise, treating the two layers as one. When you have finished pleating, make a few stitches through the net at one end to hold it together.

Sew little pearl beads or silver sequins onto the net to decorate it. Trim away any rough edges on the outside of the fan.

Finish off by spraying some round wooden beads with silver paint and sewing them to the centre of the fan to cover the pleating.

These are just as colourful as real balloons, but they won't pop, or even gently expire! Cut out balloon shapes from coloured cardboard or stiff paper, then cover them on one side with spray-on glitter.

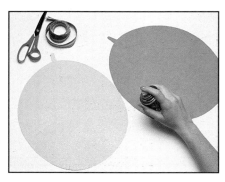

Two balloon shapes can be glued together at the edges, or they can all be strung up separately. Tape the balloons to a length of colourful striped ribbon.

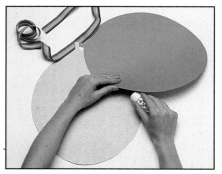

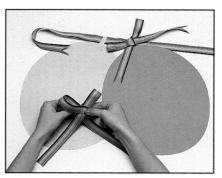

Lastly, use more of the same ribbon to make up some bows, and fix them to the balloons with some double-sided tape.

The frame for this kite is made from garden sticks. Mark off the lengths specified, and stamp on them where you want them to break! Take one stick 60cm (24in) long and another 40cm (16in) long, and tie them together with twine so that the three upper arms are equal. Next add two top pieces, 28cm (11½in) long, and the two lower side pieces 45cm (18½in) long. Tie all these in place.

Now take two large sheets of brightly coloured tissue paper. Tear one in half lengthwise and lay one half over the large sheet. Lightly glue it along the edges to keep it in place. Turn the paper over. Now lay the frame over the tissue, and cut around the shape, leaving a 5cm (2in) border all around.

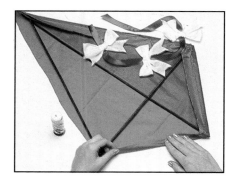

Apply glue to the outside frame of the kite, and fold the edges of the tissue over it. Finish by adding a red rosette and a paper ribbon tail with bows strung along it. After use on the big day, this can be transferred to the wall of the children's room. It has to be handled carefully, but once hung up will last for ages.

All you really need for this
decoration is some garden wire,
a little bit of tinsel and a couple of
baubles; but a pair of pliers will make
it easier to manipulate the wire. Bend
the wire into the shape of a bell.
(You could, of course, try much more
complicated shapes once you get the
hang of it.)

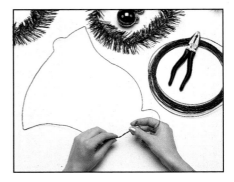

Now just wind tinsel around the wire
until it is completely covered. A
couple of layers will be sufficient.

Finish off with a bauble, tied on to
represent the clapper, and some bright
red ribbon to tie the bells together.

This is ideal for a home wedding reception. Just cut out two bell shapes from cardboard, using the template on page 119. Peel the backing off some silver sticky-backed plastic and place the cut-outs on top, pressing firmly; then cut around them.

Glue the loops at the top of the bells together, spreading the bell shapes apart as shown.

Curl some gift wrap ribbon by running the blunt edge of a scissors blade along it; attach the ribbon to the bells. Finish off with a bow tied through the loops and some tiny birds cut from foil paper. The template for these is superimposed on the bell template.

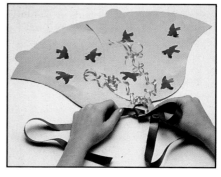

This makes an ideal Christmas wall hanging, particularly if you haven't room for a real tree. First make a paper pattern of a tree, about 75cm (30in) high and 59cm (23½in) wide at the widest point across the bottom branches. Also cut a pattern for the pot, about 25cm (10in) high. Make it about as wide as the base of the tree, with a slightly wider, 8cm (3in) deep 'rim' at the top as shown.

Cut out two pieces of green felt from the tree pattern and two pieces of red for the pot. Also cut out a piece of wadding (batting) for each. The wadding for the pot should be about 4.5cm (1¾in) shorter, since the rim of the pot will be turned down. On the front of the tree mark diagonal lines for the branches as shown.

Place the tree pieces together, with wadding on top. Pin, tack (baste), then stitch 1cm (³/8in) from the edge, leaving the lower edge open. Clip the corners and turn tree right side out. Stitch along marked lines. Make up the pot, sewing up to 4cm (1½in) from the top. Turn it right side out and slip the tree inside; sew it in place. Sew the upper sides of the pot together and turn the rim down.

To decorate the tree cut out little pockets of red felt and sew them in place as shown. Insert little gifts — either real ones or gift-wrapped cardboard squares.

Finish off by adding plenty of ribbons and bells. Curtain rings also look good covered in ribbon and sewn on. Sew a loop to the top of the tree to hang it by.

This unusual decoration adds a festive touch to a mirror or favourite painting. Make it in separate sections, one to be horizontal, the other vertical. You need fake ivy, fern and other foliage, plus pine cones, gold baubles and gold curling gift wrap ribbon. Cut off the long stems and wire everything up as shown, using florist's wire.

For the top section gradually lay pieces on top of one another, binding the wires and stems together with tape as you go along. The arrangement should be relatively long and narrow.

For the second section, use the same technique, but make the arrangement fuller. Hold the two pieces as you would like them to sit on the frame, and wire them together. Bend the stem wires back so that they will slip over the frame and hold the arrangement in place.

Hanging up your Christmas cards always poses a problem. Here is a simple way to overcome it while making an interesting 'picture' for your wall at the same time. First take a piece of wooden garden trellis, extend it, and spray it with gold paint.

While the trellis is drying, lay out some ordinary wooden clothes pegs and spray them gold as well. You will have to turn them over a few times so that all sides are covered.

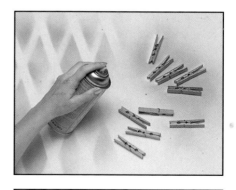

When the trellis is dry, take some thick strands of tinsel and wind them all around the edge of the trellis to make a frame. Now hang the trellis on the wall, and use the pegs to attach the Christmas cards as they arrive.

If the day outside is gloomy, try brightening the outlook with some 'stained glass window' pictures. These are cut from black art paper and backed with coloured tissue. First cut pieces of art paper 38 by 30cm (15 by 12in). Mark a 3.5cm (1½in) border all the way round. Now draw your design, taking care that it is always connected in some way to the outer border.

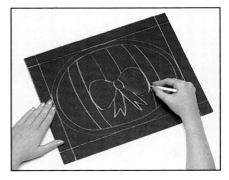

Next cut away any parts of the picture that you want to be coloured, taking care not to detach the black areas from the frame.

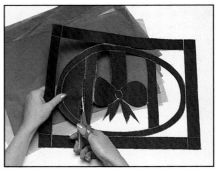

Now glue tissue paper to the back. For your first attempt use just one colour; then as you feel more confident, you can build up pictures using three or more different coloured tissues. When the picture is finished, affix it lightly to the windowpane, then watch what happens when the light shines through it.

You can always have snow at Christmas, even when the sun is shining outside. Make this snowflake in foil or in plain white paper and hang it over a window-pane. First take a square of paper, fold it into quarters, then in half diagonally, then lastly back on itself as shown.

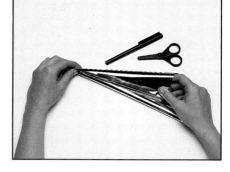

Make a pattern of the chosen design, then mark it on the folded paper with a black felt pen. Shade the areas that are to be cut away, then cut them out. Open out the snowflake. If you use a very flimsy foil, glue the snowflake onto a piece of paper, and cut out around it. This will make it easier to hang.

Finally, decorate the snowflake with sequins in bright jewel colours. The more patience you have, the more sequins you will use and the better it will look!

These little fluffy chicks make a charming mobile. For each chick you need two pom-poms (see page 127 for instructions). For the larger pom-pom use cardboard circles, 6cm (2½in) in diameter with 2.5cm (1in) holes. The small circles are 5cm (2in) across with the same size hole. When the larger one is ready to be cut away, push a pipe cleaner through the hole to form the legs and feet.

Now cut and tie the pom-poms, joining the head and body together by tying the spare yarn tightly. Make one or two stitches through the head and body to hold them in place.

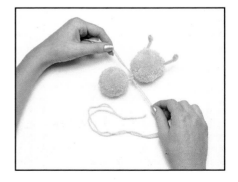

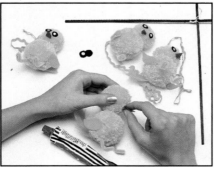

Trim each chick with a felt beak, eyes and wings, and a feather for the tail, sticking them on with a dab of glue. Tie a piece of shirring elastic around the neck, and use this to attach a piece of rickrack or ribbon to the chick. Then hang it onto two crossed sticks, tied together. Glue the rickrack in place to prevent the chicks from slipping off.

This mobile is made from cardboard (or construction paper) bird shapes with tissue paper fanned wings and tails. For each bird cut two bird shapes, using the template on page 120. Glue the two pieces together, placing thread between them, in line with the wings, to hang the bird from. Mark where the wings will fit, and cut a slit.

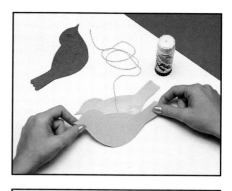

For the fanned wings take a piece of tissue paper 35 by 22cm (14 by 9in) and concertina-fold it lengthwise. Round off the edges and push the folded paper through the slit in the bird, so that there is an equal amount on each side. Glue the inside edges upward to the sides of the bird to make the wings fan out.

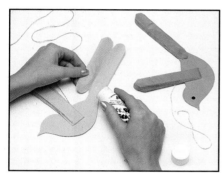

For the tail use a piece of tissue paper 35 by 12cm (14 by 5in), and concertina-fold it widthwise. Round off the edges, then slip one end over the tail of the cardboard bird; glue it in place as shown. Finish off with sequins for the eyes. Hang the birds from two crossed sticks, tied or glued together.

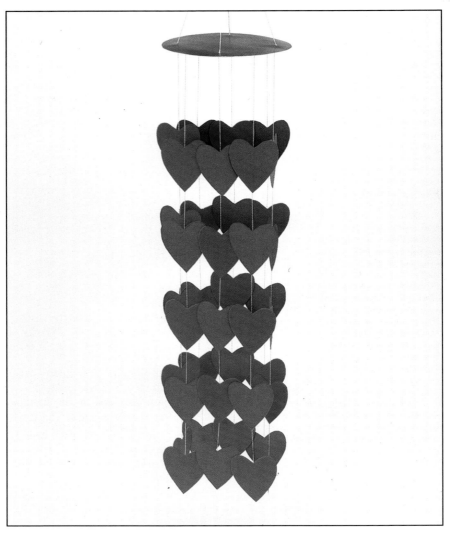

For this mobile cut out 40 hearts in thin pink cardboard and 40 in blue, using the template on page 118. Glue one side of a blue heart, lay the end of a long piece of nylon thread on it, and place a pink heart on top; press them firmly together. Now glue another two hearts together, with the thread between them, leaving a gap of about 4cm (1½in) between this and the first heart.

Add three more hearts to the thread. Cut off the thread about 20cm (8in) above the top heart. Make seven more heart strings. Cut two circles of cardboard using a dessert plate as a pattern. In one make eight tiny holes, about 2.5cm (1in) from the edge. Insert the strings and tape them in place. In the other circle insert four threads and tie them to a curtain ring. Glue the two circles together.

This tropical-style mobile is made of coloured modelling clay, the kind you can bake. You simply mould it, bake it in the oven, glue the pieces together and varnish it for a lovely shiny finish. You need eight palm trees for the mobile. Roll out the clay with a rolling pin and cut out the shape of the tree using the template on page 120.

If using more than one colour, cut the trunk and branches separately. Remember to make a hole in the top to hang each one. Also cut out a ring of clay about 15cm (6in) in diameter, with eight holes on the outer edge and four on the inner. Bake the shapes as instructed; when they are cool, glue the trunks and branches together. Varnish them on both sides.

To string them, use a strong nylon or waxed cord. The first should be 5cm (2in) long, the second 10cm (4in) and so on, with 5cm (2in) added to each length. This will give the impression that the trees fall in a spiral. Slip them through the holes in the support and knot them onto a bead above. Knot four more strings through the inner edge, and attach them to a ring to hang the mobile.

CHRISTMAS TREES

It is tempting to bring out the same tree decorations each year and use them in the same way, particularly when tree ornaments can work out so expensive. But there are many different, imaginative ways to decorate a tree, and they needn't cost the earth. In these pages you will find trees decorated in gold and silver, trees adorned with fabrics and food, green trees and frankly fake white ones. Many people object to buying a synthetic tree, but a well-made one will last for years, and won't drop needles everywhere.

We have also included plenty of ideas for individual decorations, from shiny foil bells to mini Christmas puddings.

GO FOR GOLD

This traditional tree (right) is covered in tinsel, baubles and lametta (icicles), all in gold. A similarly elegant effect could be achieved using silver on a fake white tree; or if you have a fake silver tree, try bright pink or blue. Stick to one colour only for the most professional-looking results. If the children want to hang chocolate figures on the tree, buy some colour-coordinated ones!

Start by hanging a string of white or gold lights over the tree. Lights always make the vital difference to a Christmas tree; it is lovely to switch them on when night falls. Next, trail thick gold tinsel around the branches, concealing the light cord.

The baubles can then go on, followed by strands of lametta (icicles). At the top of the tree you could place an angel or star. The star shape shown is made from loops of tinsel — simple, but very effective. The finishing touch is a pile of gold-wrapped presents at the foot of the tree. Choose some shiny wrapping paper and cover empty boxes. If you put your presents under the tree, add a few fakes too; otherwise it looks terribly bare once the presents have been opened.

This is a very pretty way to treat a synthetic white tree. The lights used are large, cone-shaped white tree lights. Next, hang on lots of baubles: pastel satin, white satin with pink bows, silver with embroidered flowers.

Now simply take lengths of pastel ribbon, such as the pink, green and blue shown here, and tie them onto the ends of the branches — some in bows, the others hanging down in strands. Tie a large bow at the top of the tree. Cover the pot or stand in silver wrapping paper, and tie a large pastel bow around it.

This is especially for the kids; but be warned: you will have to exert extreme control, or the tree will be looking very bare by Boxing Day (December 26th)! On this tree we have hung iced cookies (see the instructions on page 62), little meringues and, for the grown-ups, some Amaretti biscuits — nice with the after-dinner port!

Also hung on the tree are some cute wooden cut-outs in the shape of Santa Claus, teddy bears and other favourites. You could easily make them into a mobile after Christmas, to hang in a child's bedroom. To complete the effect, some huge gingerbread men, one at the top of the tree, some in the lower branches — perhaps too well within reach of small fingers!

Here is an unusual and very attractive way of decorating the tree, especially suitable for New Year's in Scotland. First take a set of candle lights and fasten them onto the tree. Next, you need a large bunch of gypsophilia (baby's breath). You should be able to get this all year round from a good florist.

Split up the gypsophilia and simply poke it into the tree until all the gaps between branches are filled. Although bought fresh, gypsophilia should last a few days on the tree. Next you need a piece of tartan fabric, about half a metre (yard). Cut it into strips and tie them into bows on the ends of the branches. Cover the pot or stand in coloured crepe paper and tie a large bow around it.

For a more old-fashioned look, omit sparkly baubles and lights, and stick to lace, ribbons and a few paper doilies. Start with some silk flowers wired onto the branches or simply placed on them. Take some wide lace edging and thread thin rose-coloured ribbon through the straight edge; gather it into a rosette over the ends of the branches. Allow the ends to hang down as shown.

In the gaps place some fans made from circular white paper doilies, cut in half and lightly pleated. Onto these, staple little ribbon bows, again letting the ends hang down. The pot the tree is standing in has been wrapped in plain brown paper and decorated with a large paper fan made from a rectangular doily.

These decorations are made from a basic recipe of 250g (8oz, 2 cups) plain (all-purpose) flour, 125g (4oz, 2 tablespoons) butter, 150g (5oz, ⁵/₈ cup) caster (fine granulated) sugar and 2 egg yolks. Cream butter and sugar until fluffy, add egg yolks and flour, and mix them into a firm dough. Roll the pasty out until it is about 1cm (½ in) thick, and cut out the chosen shapes.

Skewer a hole in each, so that you can push a thread through later. (This may close up during baking — in which case you will have to pierce another hole in them when they are cold — but very carefully, as the biscuits have a habit of breaking!) Put them onto a greased baking sheet, and bake them at 180°C (350°F), or gas mark 4, for 15 minutes.

When the cookies are cool, make up some fairly stiff icing using icing (confectioner's) sugar and water, and ice them. Thread them onto some waxed thread — or ribbon if the hole is big enough — and hang them on the tree straight away; they won't stay there very long!

These ornaments are very easy to make; all you need are some bells from last year's tree. If you haven't got any, look for suitable moulds in the cake decorating section of a department store. Take some ordinary granulated sugar, put a few spoonfuls in a dish, and moisten it with food colouring.

When the colouring is thoroughly mixed in, push the sugar into a bell mould, pressing it in firmly to fill the entire cavity.

Now simply tap the sugar bell out of the mould. Leave the bells to dry out overnight. To hang them on the tree, cut out a little tissue paper flower, thread a loop through it and glue it to the top of the bell. (These ornaments are not edible, and should be placed out of the reach of small children.)

These little boxes make charming tree decorations. If you haven't got any suitable ones that you can wrap for the tree, you can easily make your own from cardboard. For a cube, you need to mark out a Latin cross shape. The lower arm of the cross should be twice as long as the top and side arms. Also add a 1.5cm (½ in) border to all arms except the top one for gluing the cube together.

Fold along all the lines as shown, then bring the cube together, gluing all the sides in place.

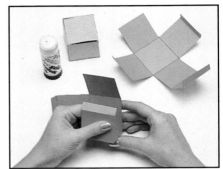

Now simply wrap the box in attractive paper, and tie it with ribbons and bows to look like a parcel. Pop it on or under the tree.

These pretty ornaments can be made any size. For a cube shape the pattern is a Latin cross (as shown), the long piece being twice the length of the others; all the other sides must be of equal length. Cut this shape out in satin, then cut a piece of iron-on interfacing, 1cm (½in) smaller all round. Iron on the interfacing. Also iron in creases to form the sides of the cube.

Placing right sides together, sew all the seams, using a small running stitch, cutting into the corners and using the interfacing edge as a seamline.

Leave one edge open so that you can turn the cube right side out. Stuff it with polyester filling, then slipstitch the opening edges together. Decorate the cube with ribbon and bows, then set it on a branch of your Christmas tree. For a rectangular box, simply widen the long section of the cross. The round box is a purchased box with satin glued onto it.

T hese jolly Santa faces will add Christmas cheer to the tree. Cut out all the pieces in felt, using the template on page 120. Glue the main face piece to a piece of cardboard. When it is dry, cut around it.

All you have to do now is glue on all the other pieces. The nose and cheeks are affixed before the moustache, which goes on top.

Place a loop of thread under the circle on the top of the hat, to hang up the face. Glue on two dark sequins to represent the eyes.

Another fun tree decoration that will last from year to year. Cut out the tree and pot in cardboard, using the templates on page 120. Now cut the shapes out in two different colours of felt, cutting two each of tree and pot. Place the two tree shapes together, and work buttonhole stitch around the edges, leaving the trunk end open.

Stuff the tree lightly with a little filling. Now buttonhole stitch around the pot, leaving the top open. Slip the trunk into the pot, and then lightly stuff the pot. Sew the tree and pot together at the sides.

Sew a little bow to the top of the pot, and decorate the tree with sequins and tinsel. Fix some gold or silver thread under the star on the top of the tree, so you can hang it up.

These miniature crackers can be hung on the Christmas tree or on the wall. First take a piece of cartridge (drawing) paper or light cardboard about 8cm (3in) wide and long enough to roll into a tube. Hold it together with a little sticky tape.

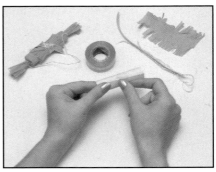

Cut a piece of crepe paper or foil twice as long as the tube, and roll the tube in it. Stick the edges together with double-sided tape. Squeeze the paper together at both ends, and tie some thread around them. Fluff out the ends and make small cuts in them to make a fringe.

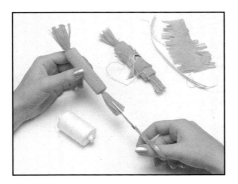

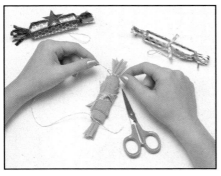

To decorate the cracker, cut some extra, narrow pieces of crepe paper or foil, fringe them at the edges and wrap them around the tube as before. Alternatively, tie a bow round the cracker or stick a silver star in the middle. Tie a length of ribbon or sparkly twine to the ends by which to hang the cracker.

Make a pattern for a Christmas stocking using the template on page 120, and cut it out double in one piece by placing the pattern on the fold of the felt. Cut a strip of fake fur to fit the stocking, about 5cm (2in) deep. Catch the fur to the felt, top and bottom, by hand, with small stitches.

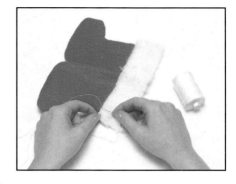

Now overcast the two sides of the stocking together, starting at the ankle and working around the foot and up the front. Turn the stocking right side out.

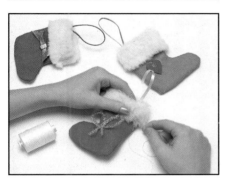

Turn the fur down about 2.5cm (1in) to the right side, catching it down around the edge. Decorate the stocking with sequins, bows, etc., and sew a loop of ribbon just inside the edge to hang it from the tree.

PING PONG PUDDINGS

Here is another cute tree decoration that is fun to make: tiny Christmas puddings. You start with ordinary ping pong balls. Spear each one onto a fine knitting needle and paint it brown. After two or three coats, for a dark rich colour, finish off with a clear varnish to give the 'puddings' a lovely shine.

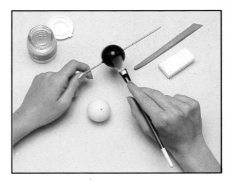

Now take some modelling clay, the sort you can bake in the oven, and roll it into a ball, the same size as the ping pong balls. Over this, mould a thick circle of white clay, to look like custard sauce. Bake this in the oven, and then remove it from the clay ball straight away, and pop it onto a pudding, so that it fits as it cools down and hardens. Don't forget to poke a hole in the top at this point.

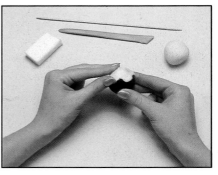

When the clay is cold, glue it to the pudding. Now take a double thread, knot the end and thread it through the pudding from the bottom upwards. Trim off the ends, then finish each pudding by gluing on foil holly leaves and red bead berries.

By the time Christmas arrives, you may not have much extra cash for Christmas tree baubles, so these colourful fakes are a great way of economizing. First cut some circles, with a little loop on the top, from some lightweight cardboard. Now mark out a pattern on each in pencil. Simple zigzags and curved lines are effective, but not too complicated to fill in.

Paint each bauble with several different colours, waiting for each to dry before painting the next. If you have some gold or silver paint, make good use of this, as it is very effective. Use black to make definite lines between colours.

When the baubles are dry, attach some thread, ribbon or, as shown, some tinsel wire, so that you can hang them up.

If you haven't any shiny bells for the Christmas tree, it's not difficult to make some from foil, beads and a little string. First take a saucer and mark around it onto the back of some coloured foil. Cut out the circle, then fold it in half, and cut along the fold line. Fold each half of the circle into a cone and glue it in place.

For the clapper, string a bead onto a length of thread — preferably waxed — and tie a knot over the bead. Lay the thread against the bell so that the clapper is at the right level, then tie a knot level with the hole in the top. This prevents the string from being pulled through the hole when threaded. Pull the string through the hole from the inside and thread on a smaller bead at the top; knot in place.

Finish each bell by dabbing a little glue around the bottom edge and sprinkling on some glitter. When you have made three bells, string them together, and attach them to a ring so that they can be hung on the tree. Wind a little tinsel wire around the string, and tie a couple of bows for that final touch of glamour.

These miniature lanterns make attractive Christmas tree ornaments. First take a piece of foil-covered paper 11cm (5½in) square. Fold it in half, and rule a line 1.5cm (¾in) from the loose edges. Now rule lines 1cm (½in) apart, from the fold up to this first line. Cut along these lines and open out the sheet of paper.

Hold the paper with the cuts running vertically, and glue the two sides together. When this is firm, set the lantern on the table and gently push the top down to make the sides poke outwards.

Finally, cut a strip of matching paper 13cm (5in) long and 1cm (½in) wide. Dab some glue on each end, and glue the strip onto the inside of the lantern, at the top, for a handle.

Ashiny foil star makes a striking decoration for the top of the Christmas tree. Using the instructions on page 35, cut out a pattern in cardboard. Now cut two squares of cardboard, slightly larger than the star template, and cover each side with a different coloured foil. Next cut out two stars, one from each foil-covered square.

Take a ruler and pencil, and placing the ruler between two opposite points, mark a line on each star from one point to the centre. Cut along these lines and then simply slot the two stars together.

Use sticky tape to hold the points together and attach a piece of green garden wire to one set of points. You can then use the wire to attach the star to the tree. Finish the star by dabbing some glue onto the points and sprinkling glitter over them for an extra-sparkly effect.

This traditional English Christmas tree-top decoration makes a charming addition to the festivities. Using a saucer, cut a circle out of silver foil paper. Cut the circle in half and fold one half into a cone, taping it in place.

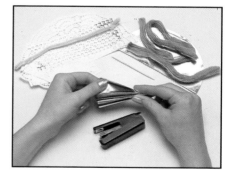

Take a pink pipe cleaner and tape it to the back of the cone; then bend it into arms and hands. On top of this fix a triangle of doily to represent wings, using double-sided tape. For the head, take an ordinary ping pong ball and skewer it onto a wooden toothpick (or cocktail stick). Push the stick into the cone.

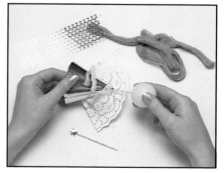

The hair is made from grey crewel or Persian wool, stuck on with double-sided tape, and the crown is a small piece of silver sequin waste. Draw the facial features with a fine-tipped silver pen. For the wand, spray a toothpick with silver paint and stick a small silver star on one end.

HATS AND MASKS

Hats are great fun to wear and to make, and the basic techniques are very useful to know, for with them you can make the headgear to go with practically any fancy dress costume. This section includes basic shapes and more complicated papier-mâché designs.

Masks are the finishing touch to any costume and can also serve as a disguise — from the sublime of a sequined ball mask to the ridiculous of a false nose, glasses and beard. And here's some useful information for making masks: the measurement from pupil to pupil is virtually the same for everyone: 6.5cm (2½in).

To make this jaunty jester's cap, first draw a graph paper pattern, using the template on page 121. The inner marked line is to be used for wadding (batting). Cut the red satin in two and place both pieces together, satin side upwards. Overlay the pattern and cut the satin double thickness, allowing a 1cm (³⁄₈in) seam allowance along the straight, centre edge.

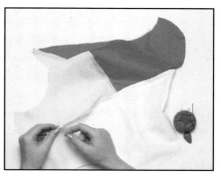

Repeat for the yellow satin. Use the main pattern against a fold to cut out two pieces of white lining fabric, and then use the smaller, inner pattern to cut two pieces of lightweight wadding (batting). Sew red and yellow sections together, then join them to the lining along the lower edge as shown. Fold the lining over the satin along the seam line, placing wrong sides together.

Slip each piece of wadding between the lining and satin, and pin all of the pieces together, with the satin on the inside. Sew them together, 1cm (³⁄₈in) from the raw edges. Turn the cap right side out, pushing out the points. Finish it by sewing a jingle bell to each point.

Feel free to act the clown in this colourful hat. First of all, make a papier-mâché mould using a pudding basin (small mixing bowl) or plastic microwave dish. (See page 124 for instructions for making papier-mâché.) When it is fully dry, remove the mould and paint it with white emulsion (water-based) paint. Sand down any rough edges and give it a second coat of paint.

Make the 'hair' from red crepe paper — you will need about six layers of paper, stapled together along the top. Cut the paper into even strips, stopping about 2.5cm (1in) from the stapled edge.

Cut out a brim from light cardboard, allowing about 5cm (2in) for the brim itself and an extra 2.5cm (1in) on the inside for attaching the brim to the crown. Make triangular cuts around the inside of the brim, fold the triangles up and glue them to the inside of the hat. Decorate with a crepe paper band and large coloured spots. Finally, glue the hair to the inside of the hat.

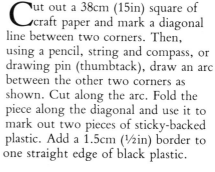

Cut out a 38cm (15in) square of craft paper and mark a diagonal line between two corners. Then, using a pencil, string and compass, or drawing pin (thumbtack), draw an arc between the other two corners as shown. Cut along the arc. Fold the piece along the diagonal and use it to mark out two pieces of sticky-backed plastic. Add a 1.5cm (½in) border to one straight edge of black plastic.

Cut out the pieces. Peel off the backing and stick the white plastic into position on the paper. Do the same with the black, leaving the backing only on the border. Form a cone, remove the border backing and stick the edges of the cone together. Make two holes along the front join and insert red pom-poms (see page 127). Secure ends on inside with tape.

For this you need a large piece of black art paper, 38 by 39.5cm (15 by 15½in). Mark a 1.5cm (½in) border at one end of the longer side so that you have a 38cm (15in) square. Take a compass, string and a white pencil and mark an arc between two corners (see page 79 for details). Cut along the arc, spread glue on the border, and use this to join the edges of the cone together.

Use the cone to mark a circle on some black cardboard. Draw another line around the first, about 5cm (2in) from it, then another just 2.5cm (1in) inside the first line. Cut along the inner and outer lines, then make triangular cuts on the inside of the brim. Fold them up and glue them to the inside of the cone. Decorate the hat with gold stars and moons cut from sticky-backed plastic.

Every would-be pirate should have one of these for dressing up! The template for the hat is on page 121. First cut out two shapes in black art paper or construction paper, and glue them together around the edges. Remember to leave the bottom edges open so that the hat can be put on!

The pattern for the skull and crossbones is superimposed on the hat template. Cut this out in silver paper and glue it to the front of the hat.

Finish the hat with a trimming of silver ribbon on the bottom of each side. For a more permanent hat, you could use felt or fabric stiffened with iron-on interfacing and sew the pieces together.

This glittery version of the medieval lady's hat, with its net veil, is sure to attract a knight errant. Cut out a 38cm (15in) square of black craft paper. Using a white pencil, string and compass, draw an arc from one corner to another. Cut along the arc.

Peel the back off some sticky-backed plastic and stick the black paper down onto it. Cut out the shape, leaving a 1.5cm (½in) border on one straight edge. Use this to stick the hat together.

Sew tinsel around the edge of a square of net, then attach this, with a little sticky tape, to the top of the hat. Make sure that the seam in the plastic is at the back. Finally decorate the hat with a few stick-on silver stars.

To make the crowns illustrated, we cheated a little by buying a pack of crown strips, which are available at some craft shops. In case you can't get them, there is a choice of templates on page 121. Cut out the crown in gold cardboard, first measuring the person's head for the length. Cut a strip of white fake fur 4cm (1½in) wide, and fix this to the crown with double-sided tape.

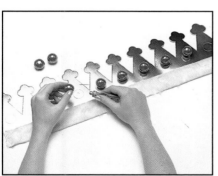

Above the fur glue fake jewels such as these painted wooden beads; if you can't get hold of any, large red sticky-backed spots will do. Now stick the two ends of the crown together with tape on the inside.

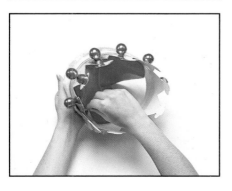

Finally, cut out a circle of red satin (draw around a large dinner plate). Put a strip of double-sided tape on the inside of the crown, and carefully pleat the satin onto it, shiny side up.

The mould for this hat is a plastic flower pot. The one shown is for a child; an adult would need a much bigger one. Cover the flower pot in papier-mâché (see the instructions on page 124). When it is dry, ease it off the pot and give it a coat of white emulsion (water-based paint), inside and out. When this is dry, sand down any rough edges on the outside and give it another coat.

Next give the hat two coats of red paint, leaving it to dry after each coat. Make a little hole in the centre of the top of the hat.

Now make a tassel of black yarn (see the instructions on page 126), and thread it through the top of the hat, fastening it on the inside with a little sticky tape.

VICTORIAN BONNET

The pattern pieces for this fetching bonnet are on page 122. From a remnant of summery fabric cut out one back crown piece, one main crown piece and two brim pieces. Also cut out the crown pieces in a plain lining fabric. Make up two crowns, one in each fabric, gathering the main pieces onto the backs. Slip the lining section into the patterned one, wrong sides together.

Cut out a paper brim, 1cm (½in) smaller than the fabric pieces all round. Glue one fabric piece to the paper brim along the outer curved edge, folding the edge of the fabric over the paper and sticking it down. Turn in and press the long edge of the other piece of fabric, and glue it on top as shown, leaving the inner edge open.

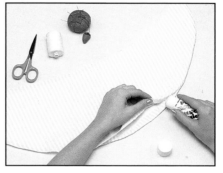

Turn in and press the inner edges of the fabric brim, clipping them as required, and press. Slip the crown inside, and slipstich the upper brim over it. On the underside, slipstich the lining over the brim. To finish, sew a lacy edging around the brim and sew ribbons and paper flowers on either side. (Instructions for paper flowers are on page 125.)

For a stunning party mask, buy a ready-moulded mask from a stationer's or toy shop. The half-mask shown here is coloured with oil stencil pencils. Start with the pink; apply a little to a piece of waxed paper, then pick it up on the stencil brush. Using a circular motion, cover about half the mask. Repeat with the blue, filling in the gaps and giving the eyes a semblance of eyeliner.

Next take a short length of lace and glue it to the back of the top half of the mask, down to where the elastic is attached. Glue some strands of curling gift wrap ribbon on either side. (Curl the ribbon by running the blunt edge of a pair of scissor along it.) Lastly, glue some large sequins over the tops of the ribbons to hide the ends, and glue another one in the centre of the forehead.

For the black mask, first sew some silver tinsel wire around the edge and around the eyes. Sew on some pearl beads either side, then sew two or three grey or white feathers under the edges for an owlish look.

MASQUE BALL

This glamorous mask is perfect for a summer ball or fancy dress party. Cut the basic shape from thin cardboard, using the template on page 122. Cover it with a fluorescent fabric, cut 1cm (½in) larger all round, clipping the edges as shown and also clipping through the eyeholes. Fold the borders over and stick them down on the reverse side.

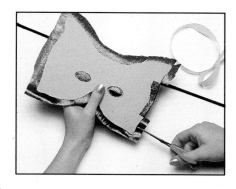

For the stick, cover a piece of garden cane with a strip of ribbon, and glue it in place. Wind fine tinsel or gold thread around it, and glue the ends down.

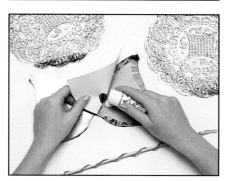

Cut a piece of gold foil paper to fit the back of the mask. Glue it down, first attaching the stick on one side. Decorate the front of the mask with sequins, feathers and pieces cut from a gold doily. If you can find only white ones in your local stores, spray a white one with gold paint.

Although a bit more complicated to make than a cardboard mask, this mask will last much longer. The face is made from papier-mâché (see page 124 for instructions); the mould is a balloon. Blow the balloon up as big as you can without bursting it, and build up the papier-mâché over at least one half. When it is dry, gently let the air out of the balloon by piercing the knotted end.

Trim the mask down, cutting the pointed end into a forehead. Cut out circular eyes and a curved mouth. Now give the mould a coat of white emulsion (water-based paint), sand it down and give it another two coats to make it as smooth a surface as possible.

Around each eye paint four slightly triangular stripes. Also paint large red lips and cheeks on either side. For the nose, paint a ping pong ball red and glue it in place. For the hair, cut short lengths of yarn and attach them to strips of sticky tape; stick these to the back of the mask. Finally, take a piece of elastic, staple it to either side, and paint over the staples with a touch more emulsion.

W ith this on, you are sure not to be recognized! First make the glasses shape from garden wire, then wind narrow ribbon all the way around them. Glue the ends in place to make sure it doesn't come undone.

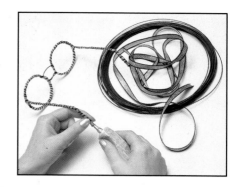

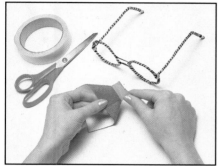

The nose is made from paper with a spongy finish. Cut a piece 9 by 10cm (3¾ by 4in). On the back, along one of the shorter sides, mark two lines, 3cm (1¼in) long and 3cm (1¼in) apart. Cut along these lines, so that you have three equal sections. Fold the two sides in and glue them on top of each other. Now glue the middle section over the others. Glue the edge of the nose to the glasses.

Finally, make the beard from a piece of white fake fur, cutting a hole for the mouth. Attach a narrow strip of paper to the inside of the nose and staple either end to the back of the beard. Finish off by sticking a silver star to the glasses, just over the nose.

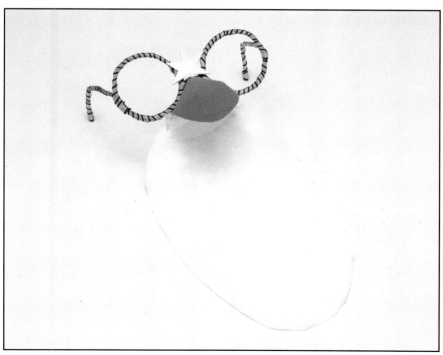

This appealing children's mask is covered in soft fake fur. Using the template on page 123, cut out the cat shape in thin cardboard, fake fur and white sticky-backed plastic. In all three, cut out the eyes.

Glue the fur piece to the cardboard one. When the glue has dried, trim the edges, then cut a nose in black felt and two ears in pink felt. To make the whiskers, put some glue onto a piece of cardboard and pull black thread through it as shown. When the thread dries it will be stiff.

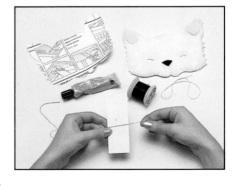

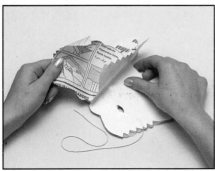

Glue the ears in place, then cut the thread into lengths of about 10cm (4in). Lay them where the nose is to be placed. Put some glue onto the nose and place it over the ends of the whiskers. Tape a piece of elastic to each side of the mask on the wrong side. Finally, peel the backing off the plastic and stick it to the underside of the mask.

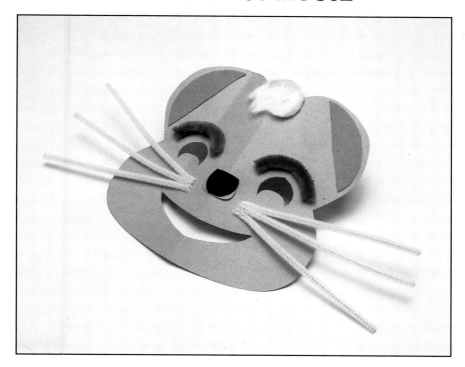

This mask is simple enough for small children to put together; the only tricky bit is drawing the pattern. First take a 20cm (8in) square of stiff paper. Fold it in half, and open it out, then fold it in half the other way. Now draw the shape of the face on one side as shown, including the mouth and nose.

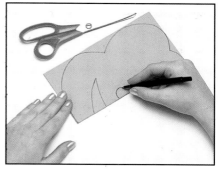

Cut around the outline, the mouth and the nose (notice that the nose isn't cut out completely). Turn back the folded edge a little way as shown; mark in an eye and cut it out. Open out the mask.

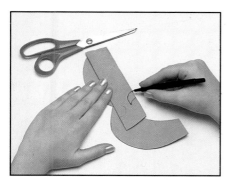

Cut out some pink felt ears and a black felt nose. Cut some white pipe cleaner whiskers and brown pipe cleaner eyebrows. Glue them all in place. Finally attach a piece of shirring elastic to either side, knotting it at the back.

To make these fake neckties, first trace a pattern from a real necktie, making the top end just under 5cm (2in) across. Then draw a wide border all around this outline. Use the pattern to cut the shape from wrapping paper. Cut an inverted 'V' through the pointed end of the border up to the point of the tie. Fold the borders over, trimming off any excess paper.

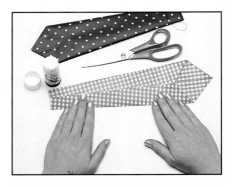

Fold under the top of the tie to hide the cut edge. Cut another piece of paper 10 by 6cm (4 by 2½in). Fold in the long edges to meet, and wrap the band around the top of the tie. Firmly crease the folds on each side.

Now remove this piece and pierce a hole in the middle of each crease. Thread a piece of shirring elastic through the hole as shown; the elastic should fit comfortably around the neck. Knot the ends of the elastic, then glue the 'knot' to the tie, with the cut edges stuck down at the back.

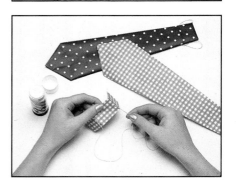

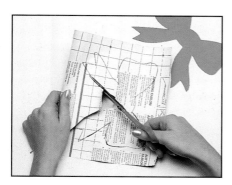

These party bow ties lend a dashing look to a costume. For the flat tie, cut a bow tie shape in thin cardboard, using the template on page 123. Simply cover the shape with foil, sticky-backed plastic or felt, and attach shirring elastic to the back.

Or make a soft fabric tie by cutting a strip of felt or other material 18cm (7in) square. Fold it in half, right sides together, and sew the long edges together to make a tube. Turn it right side out, and finish the raw edges by turning them in and slip-stitching them.

Cut another strip of material 5 by 9cm (2 by 3½in). Fold the long edges in to meet at the back and glue them down. Wrap this piece around the middle of the tube and sew it in place at the back, folding in the raw edges to hide them. Sew on shirring elastic for wearing the bow.

—— TABLE DECORATIONS ——

When you are preparing for your party, don't forget the
table. Make a spectacular centrepiece from sprayed plastic fruit,
or dried flowers, or a bouquet of fake flowers. You could perhaps add
to the fun at children's parties with personalized place cards or badges.
We have added suggestions for decorated napkins and napkin rings.

We also show you how to make your own Christmas crackers, to
suit your colour scheme and to fill with your own choice of novelties,
plus some rather special sideboard decorations, such as a ribbon tree
and a silver branch covered in spring blossoms.

This centrepiece is very effective, but simple and long-lasting. If you or any of your friends have any plastic fruit that has been sitting around for some time and is ready to be thrown away, this is the perfect opportunity to give it a new lease of life. First take a deep plastic plate and spray it gold. Next take a paper doily and spray it gold also. When they are both dry, glue the doily to the plate.

Meanwhile, take a selection of plastic oranges, apples, bananas, grapes, etc., plus some fake ivy and some pine cones, and spray them either gold or bronze. Using both colours makes for variety. Let a little of their real colour come through; it adds interest. Wind the ivy around the edge of the plate, gluing it here and there to keep it in place.

Now fill the middle with the fruit and pine cones. Again, you will have to dab a little glue here and there so that it withstands any movement.

This sort of arrangement always looks very hard to achieve, but in fact it is very simple, provided you assemble everything you need before starting. What you need is a ring of florists' foam with a plastic base, which you can get from a florist. Also buy three plastic candle holders; stick these into the foam.

You will need holly, ivy and fern, all of them either real or fake, plus a selection of dried flowers. Used here are daisy-like sunrays, yellow strawflowers or everlasting, yarrow, safflowers and sea lavender. Simply break pieces off these and stick them into the foam. Try to space the flowers evenly in between the foliage.

When you have finished, stick three candles into the holders already placed. If any of the foliage is real, make sure to keep the foam damp.

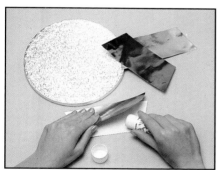

Believe it or not, this arrangement is quite simple once you get the hang of folding the cones. You need two colours of foil paper. Cut out lots of boat shapes 16.5cm (6½in) along the top and 12.5 (5in) along the bottom and about 6cm (2½in) deep. Glue one colour to another, back-to-back.

Form each boat into a cone and glue it in place. The first few you make may not look too professional, but it doesn't matter; these can go on the outside of the stand and will be partially covered. You will soon get the hang of folding the cones. Bend the bottoms under; it helps to hold the shape and looks tidier.

When you have several cones made, start gluing them around the edge of a 20cm- (8in-) diameter silver cake board. Place another two layers inside the first, leaving room for a chunky candle in the middle.

What could be prettier than this profusion of ribbons and flowers? The one shown is pink and white, but you should choose whatever matches your décor. First of all you will need a biscuit or cake tin. Cover the outside with silver foil paper, allowing a little extra at the top to turn over and glue. (This will be easier if you snip down to the tin.) Decorate it with strips of ribbon.

Take a block of florists' foam and cut it to fit inside the tin, using the extra bits to fill in the gaps around it.

Now wire up pieces of gift wrap ribbon, little baubles, strips of crepe paper and silk flowers. Curl the ribbon by running the blunt edge of a pair of scissors along it. Push the wires into the foam, arranging them until the tin is totally full. Use strips of ribbon around the outside, and let them fall over the side of the tin.

The sideboard, as well as the table, needs a little dressing up at Christmas. This is bright and cheery, and the materials are quite easy to get hold of. If you don't have woodland nearby your florist should have small sections of bark for sale. Also buy a plastic candle holder. Onto the bark first put a large lump of green Plasticine (modelling clay), and on the top stick your candle holder.

Now take some plastic or silk fern and spray it gold. Break off pieces when it is dry, and stick them into the Plasticine. Also wire up strands of red paper ribbon, pine cones and red baubles and stick these in.

When the Plasticine is artistically concealed, pop a red candle in the holder, and set the arrangement on the sideboard. Put a mat under it, though, or it will scratch the surface.

Spring is in the air, with a shiny silver pot plant, blossoming with pink silk flowers. You need a small plastic pot and a small, graceful tree branch. Spray them both with silver paint.

Now take a block of Plasticine (modelling clay), weighting the base with a stone if necessary. Push the silver branch into the middle and fix the Pasticine into the pot. For the 'earth' scrunch up a piece of silver foil and arrange it around the branch.

For the blossoms you need little pink silk flowers, scrunched up pink tissue, green tissue leaves and pink and green gift wrap ribbon. Glue these along the branch as shown, spacing them so as to look reasonably realistic.

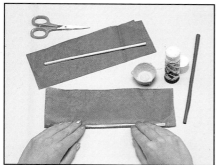

Make some spring flowers that will bloom throughout the year. For the base of each daffodil head, cut a section from an egg box and trim it down to an even edge. Use a yellow one if you can, or else paint it yellow. Next take a flexible paper or plastic straw and roll it in a strip of green tissue, gluing both long edges. Trim the ends and bend the straw without tearing the paper.

Cut out some yellow tissue petals and glue first one row, then a second, around the inside of the egg box base.

Finally, scrunch up a small piece of orange tissue paper and glue it to the centre of the flower.

If you have no room for a proper Christmas tree, this would be a good alternative — small but spectacular. First take a medium-sized plastic flower pot, about 15cm (6in) in diameter, and fill it, up to about 2.5cm (1in) from the rim, with fast-drying cement or wood filler. When this is just setting, insert a piece of 1.5cm (½in) dowelling about 40cm (16in) long.

When the filler is dry, spray paint the pot, the dowelling and the 'earth' surface gold. Lay it down to spray it, and when one side is dry, roll it over and spray the other side. The whole thing — especially the pot — will need a couple of coats.

When the paint is dry, take a ball of florists' foam at least 12cm (5in) in diameter and push it on top of the dowelling.

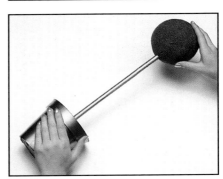

Now take short lengths of deep red and green satin ribbon, gold ribbon, shiny baubles and gold tinsel, and wire them all up, ready to push into the foam. Start with about a dozen of each; you can add to them as you go along, if necessary.

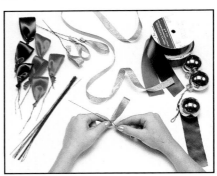

Start inserting the wires into the sphere, arranging the ribbons and baubles until it is covered, with no foam showing through. Finally wire up some curling gift wrap ribbon and insert it into the bottom of the ball. (Curl the ribbon by running the blunt edge of a pair of scissors along it.) Wind gold tinsel around the 'trunk' of the tree, and tie a large bow around the pot as a finishing touch.

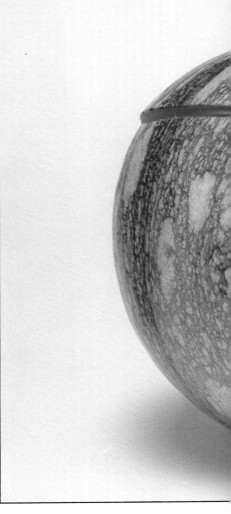

A pumpkin is a versatile vegetable; use one to make this jolly Halloween lantern and some good things to eat also. First take a ripe pumpkin and cut a slice off the top. You will need a very sharp knife, as pumpkins can be very tough — so be careful of your fingers.

Scoop out the insides, leaving a good 1 to 2.5cm (½ to 1in) rind. Use the flesh to make a pumpkin pie. The seeds also can be eaten. Wash and dry them, then place them on a baking tray and sprinkle them with salt. Bake them in the oven until they are dry and crunchy.

Now mark the eyes, nose and mouth on the front of the pumpkin with a black felt pen.

Cut carefully around the lines, and then push the features out from the inside. Rinse out the inside of the pumpkin, and dry it thoroughly with paper towels.

Finally, pop a couple of night lights or small candles inside, light them, and put the top on the pumpkin. Place the jack-o'-lantern on a window sill to frighten away any spooks.

These most unusual flowers are made from coloured nylon stockings or tights (pantyhose). First cut some pieces of copper wire 20cm (8in) long. Bend each into a petal shape with pliers. You need five petals for each flower. Cut the nylons into pieces and stretch them over the wire very tightly, binding them on with green tape.

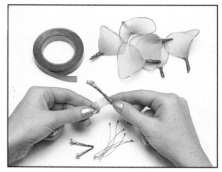

Take five stamens (obtainable from craft shops), bend them in half and use pliers to attach them to the end of a long piece of copper wire, again binding them with green tape.

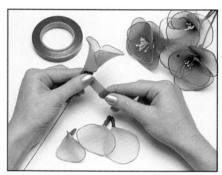

Now arrange the petals around the stamens. Start by placing the middle two opposite each other. Bind them, then add the other three around them. When all the petals are in place, tape around the top of the stem and continue down it to the end. When you have made several blooms, wrap them in shiny paper and tie a net bow around the outside.

GLAMOUR CRACKER

This beautiful cracker is not designed to be pulled but to be taken home as a memento. First take a tube of cardboard and wrap white crepe paper around it. Insert short cardboard tubes into each end, leaving gaps of 5cm (2in) between the main and end sections. Cover the central and end sections on the outside with silver foil paper, and stick pink foil paper to the inside of the end sections.

Wind a length of silver sequin waste around the centre. Next take two strips of pink net and draw a piece of thread through the centre of each to gather it. Tie them at each end with a strip of curling gift wrap ribbon. (Curl the ribbon by running the blunt edge of a pair of scissors along it.)

Finish by decorating the cracker with large sequins and a pink foil heart, or with some other shape if you prefer. If you like, pop a little gift inside — a hand-made chocolate, perhaps, or even a diamond ring!

Christmas crackers are very simple to make yourself, and you can fill them with gifts of your own choosing. First take a piece of crepe paper 36 by 16cm (14 by 6in). On top of this, glue a piece of lining paper 30 by 14cm (12 by 5in). On top of this, place a cracker snap; in some countries you can buy packs of snaps, mottos, etc., from party shops near Christmastime.

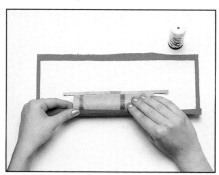

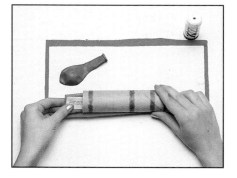

Next take a piece of cardboard tubing and glue it to the centre of one edge as shown.

When the glue has dried, slip a paper hat, motto or joke and gift inside the tube.

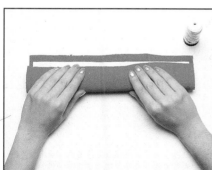

Dab some glue along the other long side, then roll the tube inside the paper.

Squeeze the ends of the paper and slip an elastic (rubber) band over each for a few moments to hold them in. Take them off when you are ready to decorate the cracker. To do this use ribbon, lace, stars, leaves, etc. Pieces of gold doily also look very effective stuck onto the front of a cracker.

To make this simple gift for the table, fill a paper cone with chocolate drops or jellies for a children's party, or with sugared almonds for grown-ups. All you need is a small square of brightly coloured wrapping paper, a ribbon rosette, and some tissue paper. Simply roll the paper into a cone from corner to corner, taping it into a nice rounded shape.

Flatten the cone slightly, positioning the top point in the centre; then fold up the bottom and stick on the ribbon rosette.

Scrunch up a little bit of tissue paper and slip it inside the cone to hold it in shape, then fill the top with sweets so that they spill out onto the point. You could attach a place card to each cone and use the cones to mark place settings at a large party.

These are cute little gifts to place beside each setting on the table. Begin by cutting out a circle of net, using a standard sized dinner plate as a guide.

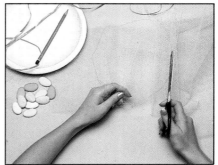

Place a few pastel-coloured sugared almonds into the net, and bunch it into a parcel with an elastic (rubber) band to hold it together.

Now just trim the parcel with curling gift wrap ribbon. (Curl the ribbon by running the blunt edge of a pair of scissors along it.) You could slip a name tag over the ribbon before tying it and use the parcel as an unusual place marker.

To make one of these pretty baskets you will need a sheet of paper 20cm (8in) square. Fold the square in half diagonally, then diagonally again. Place the triangle with the single fold running vertically. Bring the upper of the two free points up to meet the single point, opening the flap out as you do so to form a square. Crease the folds and repeat on the other side.

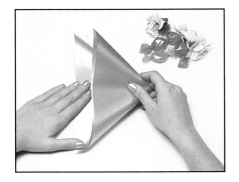

Position the newly formed square with the free edges pointing away from you. Fold the top free corner down to meet the opposite corner, then fold it back on itself to the horizontal centre line. Fold the flap in half once more. Repeat on the other side as shown. Turn the top left flap over to the right side, then fold it back on itself so that the corner meets the vertical centre line.

Fold the left hand corner in towards the vertical centre line also. Turn the basket over and repeat on the other side as shown. Open out the shape slightly and fold the top two flaps down inside the basket. Flatten the base. Cut a thin strip of paper for a handle and slip the ends into the slots on each side of the basket rim. Staple in place and decorate the basket with ribbons or lace.

This cute little rabbit can be popped over a soft-boiled egg to keep it warm. First cut out two rabbit shapes in white felt, using the template on page 123. Cut the ears from pink felt, the waistcoat from yellow, and the nose and eyes from black. Glue them in place. Embroider the mouth and whiskers in black thread. Glue on sequins for the buttons and for the whites of eyes.

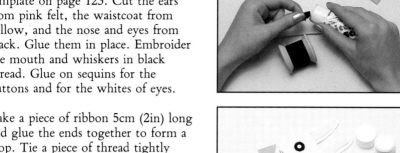

Take a piece of ribbon 5cm (2in) long and glue the ends together to form a loop. Tie a piece of thread tightly around the middle of the ribbon to form a bow, and sew it to the rabbit between the mouth and the top of the waistcoat.

With wrong sides facing, sew the front and back together along the edge, using blanket stitch.

To break the ice at a kids' party — iced cupcake name badges. The template for the pieces is on page 123. Cut each cake shape from thin cardboard as a base for the felt. Then cut out the top and bottom pieces, again in cardboard.

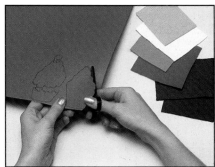

Glue the latter pieces to different colours of felt and cut around them. Now glue these separate pieces to the base card.

Finish off by sticking a name label to the front of the bun and a little double-sided tape to the back. When the little guests arrive simply tear off the backing from the tape and label them!

TEDDY BEARS' PICNIC

Teddy not only tells the little ones where to sit, but can be taken home afterwards as a little party gift. Draw a teddy shape using your favourite bear as inspiration and folding the paper at the top to produce a double shape as shown. Cut the shape from a spongy textured paper or from felt. Now glue this to some brown cardboard and carefully cut around it.

Now cut out two yellow circular tummies, some pink ears and paws — the forepaws slightly smaller than the back ones — black and white eyes and black noses, all from felt. The mouth is a tiny piece of black yarn. Glue all these in place.

Fold the teddies in half across the ears, and stick a label on each tummy with the child's name written on it.

H ere are a couple of ideas for jazzing up ordinary paper napkins. For the blue napkin, cut a star shape from a piece of cardboard — the cardboard must be slightly wider than the folded napkin. Hold the cardboard firmly in place over the napkin and spray silver or gold paint over the area. Let the paint dry for several minutes before you allow anything else to touch it.

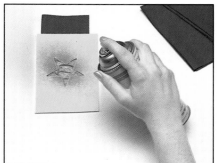

The white napkins have a design stencilled on them with oil-based stencil crayons. You can buy these separately or in packs, with ready-cut stencils. Choose your design, then place it over the area you want to stencil — in this case the corner of the napkin. Rub the crayon over a spare area of stencil, then take the colour up onto the brush and paint it over the stencil, in a circular motion.

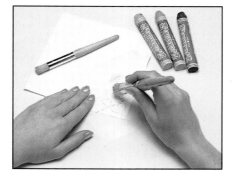

Use the brush only over the parts you wish to show up in that colour. Now switch to the next colour. It is best to use a different brush for each colour if you want clear colour definition.

For a bit of fun at Christmastime, make some especially festive napkin rings. Each is made from a piece of cardboard tubing. The leaf sprig ring is first covered with a strip of sticky-backed plastic. Cut the plastic wide enough to go over to the inside of the ring, and cover the inside with a thinner strip of ribbon. The leaf design is a Christmas cake decoration.

Another ring has a strip of fake fur stuck to the outside, to represent snow, and green felt to disguise the cardboard on the inside. Top it with a tiny green felt Christmas tree, sparkling with sequins.

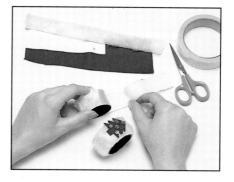

Still another idea is to cover the ring with a small strip of wide satin ribbon. Glue a piece of narrower toning ribbon to the inside, folding the edges of the wide ribbon under as you go. Lastly, tie a strand of tinsel wire around the ring and finish with a bow.

TEMPLATES AND TECHNIQUES

Some of the projects in this book are based on the templates given on the next six pages. These have been reduced in size, in order to fit the space available; so you will first need to enlarge them. If, for example, each square of the printed grid is said to represent 5cm (2in), you should first rule a grid containing the same number of squares, but making them 5cm (2in) square. Then, using the grid lines as a guide, copy the shape onto your full-size grid.

On pages 124-127 you will find step-by-step instructions for some basic 'ingredients' required in many party decorations.

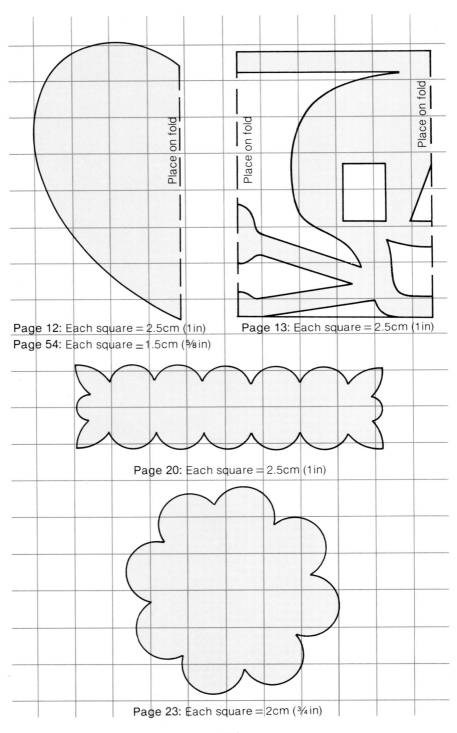

Page 12: Each square = 2.5cm (1in)
Page 54: Each square = 1.5cm (⅝in)

Page 13: Each square = 2.5cm (1in)

Page 20: Each square = 2.5cm (1in)

Page 23: Each square = 2cm (¾in)

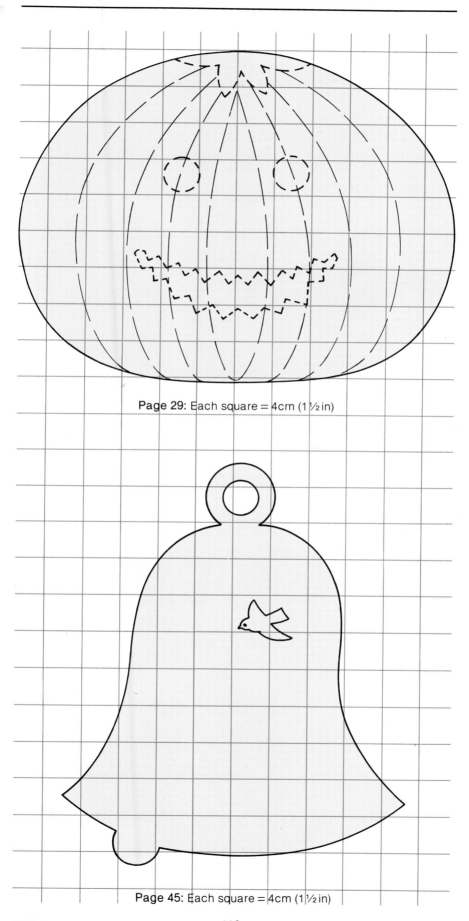

Page 29: Each square = 4cm (1½in)

Page 45: Each square = 4cm (1½in)

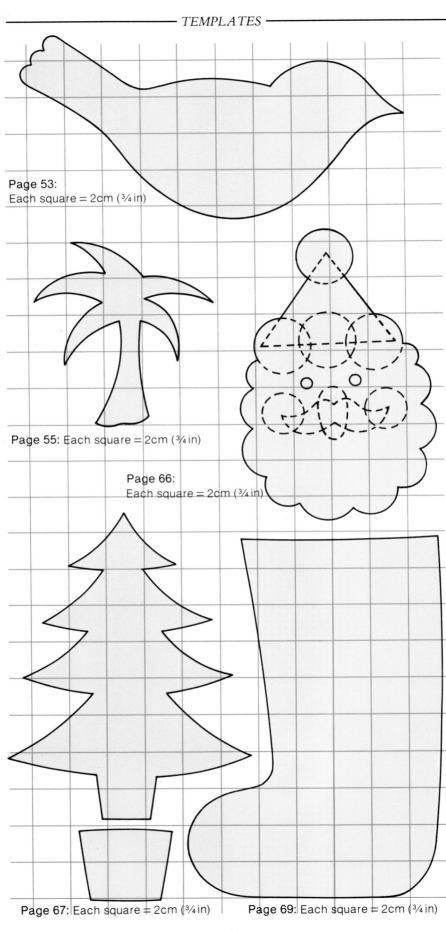

Page 53:
Each square = 2cm (¾ in)

Page 55: Each square = 2cm (¾ in)

Page 66:
Each square = 2cm (¾ in)

Page 67: Each square = 2cm (¾ in)

Page 69: Each square = 2cm (¾ in)

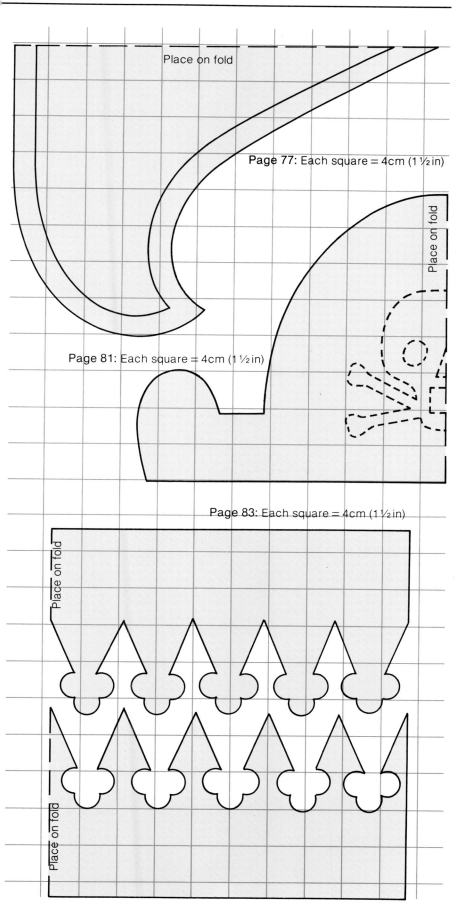

Place on fold

Page 77: Each square = 4cm (1 ½ in)

Place on fold

Page 81: Each square = 4cm (1 ½ in)

Page 83: Each square = 4cm (1 ½ in)

Place on fold

Place on fold

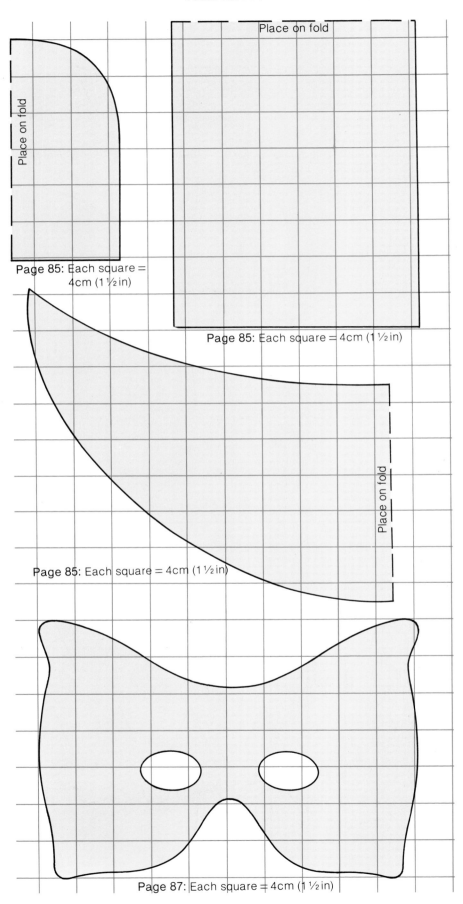

Place on fold

Place on fold

Page 85: Each square = 4cm (1½ in)

Page 85: Each square = 4cm (1½ in)

Place on fold

Page 85: Each square = 4cm (1½ in)

Page 87: Each square = 4cm (1½ in)

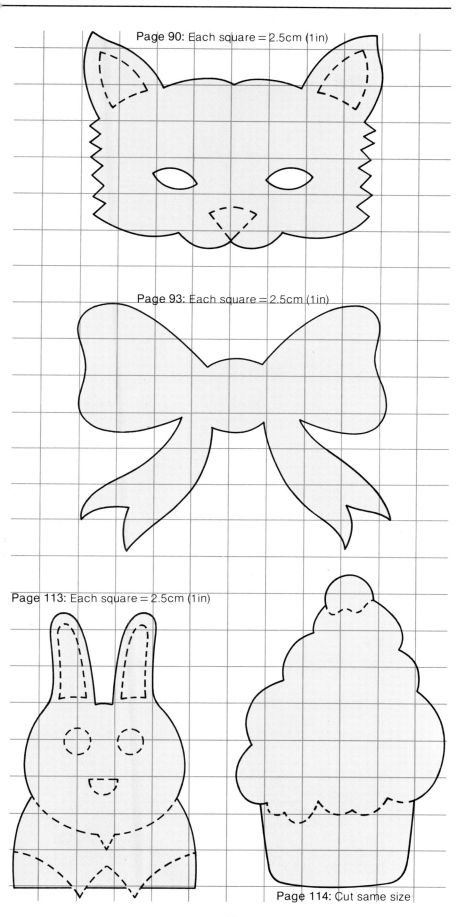

Page 90: Each square = 2.5cm (1in)

Page 93: Each square = 2.5cm (1in)

Page 113: Each square = 2.5cm (1in)

Page 114: Cut same size

This is something we probably all learned at school but many of us have long forgotten! First you need to choose a bowl or some other receptacle that is roughly the shape you wish to achieve. Tear up lots of newspaper into narrow strips, and then make up a flour and water paste, not too stiff, not too runny. You will soon discover the correct consistency when you get started.

Dip the newspaper into the paste and start placing it on the bowl, working your way around it until the whole surface is covered. Keep working over it, in all directions, until you have built up at least six layers. This will give you a firm mould. Make sure to keep it smooth as you go along.

When you have finished, leave the papier-mâché to dry in a warm dry place. It will take about 24 hours to dry completely — more if it is particularly thick. When it is ready, ease it off the bowl. You may have to sand down the rough edges, but this is best done after the first coat of paint, as this will show up any lumps and bumps.

These little carnation-shaped flowers are useful for adorning all sorts of decorations, or can be used by themselves to make a lovely floral centrepiece. Take an ordinary paper tissue and cut it in half lengthwise. Concertina-fold it down its length, as shown, then tie it in the middle with a piece of wire or twine.

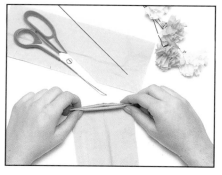

Fold the tissue in half, and wrap one end of the wire firmly around the base to hold the shape in position. (The other end serves as the stem.)

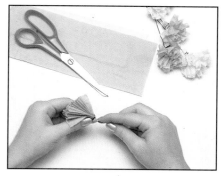

Now simply fluff out the paper, teasing it with your fingers until it resembles a carnation.

T assels are useful for trimming hats or the edges of hanging decorations, and they are very easy to make. Cut several strands of yarn or cord; the more you cut, the fuller the tassel will be. The strands should be twice the finished length of the tassel. Tie them firmly in the centre. Leave the tying strands uncut, and fold the tassel strands in half.

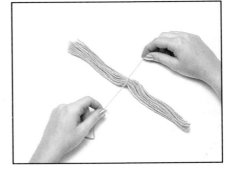

Now wind a cord several times around all the strands, about 2.5cm (1in) from the top (or less, for a small tassel.) Tie it firmly and cut off the ends.

Trim the ends off the tassel so that they are all the same length. Use the top cord to attach it to whatever you are trimming.

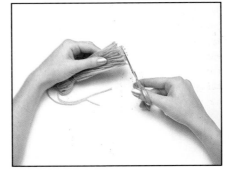

These jolly trimmings, ideal for party hats, can be made of yarn left over from knitting projects. First cut two circles of cardboard with a diameter the size you wish the finished pom-pom to be. Cut a fairly large hole in the centre. Now wind yarn (doubled, to speed up the work) over the cardboard rings until you can barely push the yarn through any more.

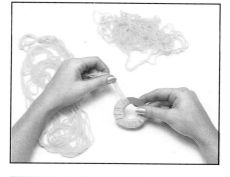

The more yarn you use, the bushier the pom-pom. When you have finished, tie off the end of the yarn. Snip through all the yarn around the outer edge of the cardboard rings.

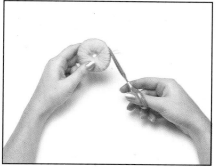

Wind a piece of yarn between the cardboard rings around all the strands. Pull firmly and make a strong knot, leaving long ends. Now take out the rings. Finish by trimming off any straggling ends of yarn.

INDEX

ACKNOWLEDGEMENTS

The author and publishers would like to thank the following for their help
in compiling this book:

Valley Industries Ltd., 5 Heathermount Drive, Crowthorne, Berkshire

Porth Decorative Products Ltd., Tonypandy, Mid Glamorgan, Wales

Philip and Tacey Ltd., North Way, Andover, Hants

Offray Ribbons Ltd., Ashbury, Rosecrea. Co. Tipperary, Ireland
(UK office: Fir Tree Place, Church Rd., Ashford, Middlesex)

Naylor Ball Design Partnership, 177 Waller Rd., London SE14

Fablon, the House of Mayfair, Cramlington, Northumberland

Special thanks also go to Marion Dale and Pearl Piggot